**BATH – MACMILLAN
SCIENCE 5–16**

Transporters

First edition 1991

Published by
MACMILLAN EDUCATION LTD
Houndmills, Basingstoke, Hampshire RG21 2XS
and London
Companies and representatives throughout the world

Designed by Fox and Partners

Printed in Great Britain by Butler & Tanner Ltd, Frome and London

British Library Cataloguing in Publication Data
Transporters: pupil's book
1. Physics. Transport phenomena
I. Series
530.475
ISBN 0–333–53077–2

The Project Team

The *Bath-Macmillan Science 5-16* Project Team is directed by Professor Jeff Thompson CBE and Dr Martin Hollins of the University of Bath School of Education. The principal authors for the Key Stage 3 materials were:

Ralph Levinson	Christine Harrison	Marcus Barbor
Pete Richardson	Miriam Chaplin	Mary Doherty
Allan Covell	John Harris	Helena McVeigh

with support from Janet Major, John Collins, Chris Richardson, Lesley Stone and Richard Swan. *Transporters* was written by Miriam Chaplin, with support from Martin Hollins.

Acknowledgements
The authors and publishers wish to acknowledge, with thanks, the following photographic sources: Bryan and Cherry Alexander p. 36; All-Sport Photographic Ltd pp. 10, 11 bottom left, 16, 19 left; British Airways p. 11 bottom right; Jim Brownbill p. 11 top right; J Allan Cash Photo Library pp. 11 centre right, 17, 19 right, 21; Colorsport p. 13; L.S. & A International p. 20; Ministry of Defence title page; NASA p. 28; Picturepoint p. 8; Science Photo Library pp. 24, 35, 40; Alan Thomas pp. 7, 11 top left, 11 centre left, 15, 18 bottom; Topham Photo Library cover, p. 26; Transport and Road Research Laboratory p. 18 top; Zefa (UK) Ltd p. 14.

Illustrations drawn by: Craig Warwick pp. 4/5, 9 bottom, 12, 17, 22/23, 37; Tek Art pp. 6/7, 10, 14 bottom, 16, 19, 20 bottom, 31 right, 34, 36; Fox and Partners pp. 8, 9 top, 14 top, 35; Gillian Hunt p. 20; Mile Gornall pp. 24, 26, 28, 30, 30/31, 32, 33 bottom; Gary Bines pp. 27, 33 top, 38 top, 39.

The authors and publishers are grateful for advice and assistance from Nick Selley, Trevor Roach, Dave Headey and the School Science Service, CLEAPSS.

The publishers have made every effort to trace the copyright holders, but where they have failed to do so they will be pleased to make the necessary arrangements at the first opportunity.

TRANSPORTERS

Contents

Unit 1 Learner drivers	4
Unit 2 Measuring movement	9
Unit 3 Safe journeys	17
Unit 4 Providing the power	21
Unit 5 The Mars Mission: getting ready	24
Unit 6 The Mars Mission: arrival and return	33

UNIT 1
LEARNER DRIVERS

Section 1.1
HOW DO WE TRAVEL?

How did you come to school today? In which of the forms of transport shown in the pictures have you travelled?

Most people enjoy travelling. All over the world, more people are travelling than ever before and people are also travelling further. Newspapers are full of advertisements for all kinds of travel; there are holiday packages using charter aeroplanes, trains and coaches; there are new kinds of bicycles, motor cycles and cars.

Newspapers also report on the problems that all this travelling can produce: petrol exhaust fumes cause pollution; the world's resources of oil and metal are being used up rapidly; holiday-makers have to wait for hours in overcrowded airports or in motorway traffic jams and there are dangers of accidents and hijacks. These problems can make people unhappy about travelling.

Discuss

- Do you have a favourite way of travelling?

- What vehicle would you buy if you could afford it?

- Are there any ways you don't like to travel? Why is this?

- Which methods of travelling cause least harm to the natural environment?

Section 1.2
MAKING THINGS MOVE

In this unit you will be investigating some of the ways in which vehicles are made to move and to stop moving. You will be using models and toys because this is more convenient than the real thing (it is also cheaper and safer!).

Investigate

- Carry out one or more of the following investigations. Make notes in your book as you do each investigation to answer these questions.

  1 How did you get the vehicle to move?

  2 How does it work?

  3 What can you change to make it go faster?

  4 What is a good way to stop it when you want it to stop?

  5 What may happen if it can't stop?

  When you have finished your investigation be ready to explain to the other groups in your class what you have found out.

A Push-pull trucks

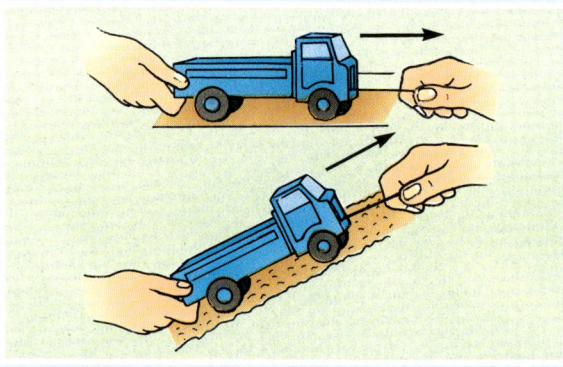

- Move the truck along the bench by pushing it with one hand and pulling it with the other hand using a rubber band or a piece of elastic.

- Try different slopes and different surfaces for it to run on, and different loads for it to carry.

B Cars with engines

- Make the car move along the bench using the 'engine'.

  If it has an electric motor – switch it on.

  If it is a clockwork car – wind it up.

  If it has a flywheel inside – wind it up by moving the car backwards on the bench.

- Try to make the car move along different slopes and different surfaces.

C Electric and magnetic trains

- Use rubber bands or string to fix one magnet to an engine and another magnet to one of the carriages.

- Make the carriage move by bringing the engine close to it but without touching it.

  Can you make the carriage move in a different direction by changing the magnet round on either the carriage or the engine?

- If you have an electric train, switch it on and find out how its movement can be changed using the controls.

D Paddle and propeller boats

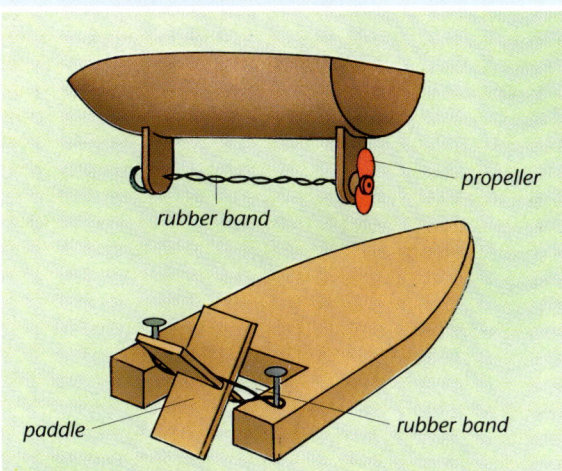

- Make each of the boats move by winding up the elastic and releasing it.

Is one method (paddle or propeller) better than the other?

How could you test this?

E Propeller and jet aeroplanes

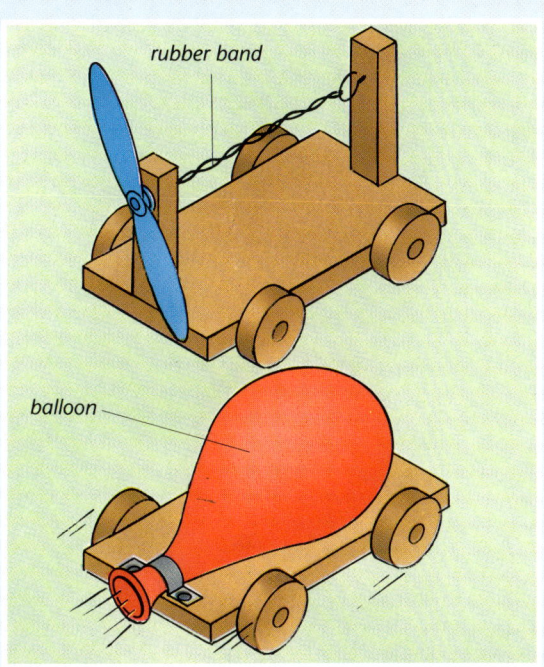

- Aeroplanes are driven by jets or propellers. It is easier to investigate how they work if they can move on land, so wheels have been put on these aeroplane models. Make the 'propeller' aeroplane move by winding up the elastic and then releasing it. Make the 'jet' aeroplane move by blowing up the balloon and then releasing the air from it.

Is one method better than the other?

Section 1.3
GOING FOR A RIDE

All of the vehicles you investigated and learnt about in Section 1.2 were driven by different forces.

Discuss

- What kinds of forces were used to drive them?

- What difference does a big force make compared to a small one?

- What forces were used to slow down the vehicles?

- The lorry in the picture has gone out of control and crashed. What have the forces caused by the crash done to the lorry and to the things it has crashed into?

- What could you change to make the crash do less damage?

It is very important to be able to control the movement of vehicles. This usually means controlling the forces. This makes travelling in the vehicles safer and more comfortable.

Think about

- Imagine you are a passenger in one of the toy vehicles that you investigated in Section 1.2. Write a story about how it would feel to travel in it, along a winding, bumpy road.

- Look again at the vehicles shown in the picture on pages 4–5. Think about how they move. Choose one vehicle and write down the things which help people to travel in it safely and comfortably.

UNIT 2
MEASURING MOVEMENT

Section 2.1
HOW FAST IS IT?

People have always been interested in getting things to move faster and in who could run the fastest. This raises the problem of how to decide fairly!

Plan and test

- In your group, discuss how you could carry out a fair test to find out which one of you can run the fastest.

- Tell your teacher what you plan to do. When your plan has been approved, carry out your test.

- Present your results to the rest of the class.

Stacey, Elif and Ben have just finished building their buggies and they want to know whose is 'best'. They have decided to find out which is the fastest!

Plan and test

- In your group, discuss how you could carry out a fair test to find out which is the fastest buggy.

- Explain to your teacher what you plan to do. When your plan has been approved, carry out the test with your own buggies or with clockwork toys.

- Present your results to the rest of the class.

Section 2.2
RUNWAYS

Grand Prix drivers have to be experts at controlling the speed of their cars; this photograph shows Nigel Mansell driving a Ferrari at the 1990 British Grand Prix

Controlling speed is an important skill for motorists and for scientists too. In later investigations you will be studying the forces needed to stop cars at different speeds and the effects of crashes at different speeds. In order to do this you need to be able to make a car travel at different speeds. This short investigation will help you find out what things affect the speed of a toy car rolling down a slope.

Investigate

• Set up a runway as shown in the diagram, with just a gentle slope to it. It is a good idea to use a long runway if you can.

• Plan how you will carry out one of the following investigations. Check with your teacher which one you should do.

(a) Investigate how the height of the top edge of the runway affects how quickly cars roll down the slope.

(b) Investigate how the height of the top edge of the runway affects the average speed of cars.

Remember to consider the following points when planning your investigation:

How will you make it a fair test?

What will you need to measure?

Would it be best to present the results as a table, a bar chart or in some other way?

• Carry out your investigation and record your results.

• Present a report of your investigation to the rest of the class.

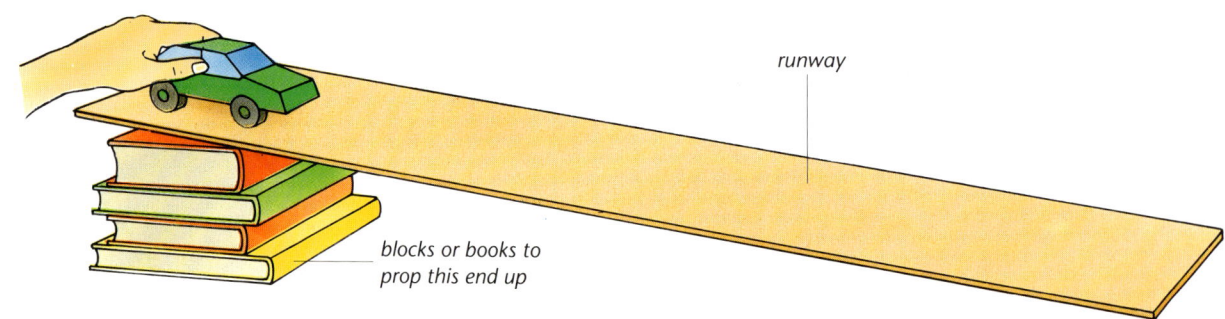

runway

blocks or books to prop this end up

Section 2.3
A SENSE OF SPEED

How good are you at estimating speed?
This activity will help you find out.

Think about

• These photographs show things travelling at different speeds. Estimate how fast each one is moving by choosing what you think is the best answer to each of the questions. Two of the questions have already been answered to help you with the others.

Does Jeremy, the fastest snail in the garden, have an average speed of 1 centimetre per second, 20 centimetres per second or 1 metre per second?
(*Best answer* 1 centimetre per second)

Does a world class sprinter run at 2 metres per second, 10 metres per second or 50 metres per second?
(*Best answer* 10 metres per second)

Does an InterCity train, on a straight, fast track, travel at 20 metres per second, 30 metres per second, 50 metres per second or 100 metres per second?

Florence Griffith-Joyner at the US Olympic Trials 1988

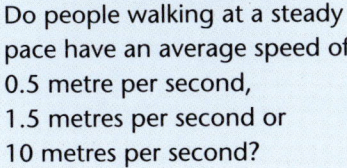

Do people walking at a steady pace have an average speed of 0.5 metre per second, 1.5 metres per second or 10 metres per second?

In fast-moving town traffic, do vehicles travel at 2 metres per second, 15 metres per second, 30 metres per second or 50 metres per second?

Does Concorde cruise at 60 metres per second, 600 metres per second or 60 000 metres per second?

In the UK the speed of cars, trains and other vehicles is usually measured in miles per hour (m/h or m.p.h.) but in most other countries, and in science, technology and industry, speed is measured in metres per second (m/s) or kilometres per hour (km/h).

To find the average speed of something, we divide the distance it travels by the time it takes to travel that distance.

Here is an example:

distance travelled = 100 metres
time taken = 20 seconds

$$\text{average speed} = \frac{\text{distance travelled}}{\text{time taken}}$$

$$= \frac{100 \text{ metres}}{20 \text{ seconds}}$$

$$= 5 \text{ metres per second}$$

Work out

• The table gives the times and the distances covered by competitors in several track (running) events. For each event, write down the competitors' names in finishing order, with the fastest first and the slowest last.

Name of Competitor	Event	Time taken
Jeff	100 m	15 s
Marianne	100 m	13 s
Richard	100 m	11 s
Wendy	100 m	12 s
Trusha	200 m	23 s
Darshana	200 m	30 s
Kerziban	200 m	25 s
Ashish	200 m	26 s
Ameet	400 m	100 s
Sean	400 m	80 s
Lewis	400 m	95 s
Stavronlla	400 m	120 s

Who was the fastest runner in each event?

Who was the fastest runner overall? Explain your answer.

Work out   EXTRA!

• Copy this table into your book and complete it by calculating the average speeds.

Distance travelled	Time taken	Average speed
100 km	2 h	
50 km	2 h	
100 m	20 s	
400 m	20 s	

Section 2.4
STARTING

*How much force do you think this man is
using to pull the van?*

Things tend to stay where they are unless something or someone pushes or pulls them. We are going to find out if the mass of an object affects the size of the force needed to get it moving. Force is measured in newtons (N). We use a newtonmeter to measure force; this is just a spring balance marked in newtons.

Investigate

- Use a newtonmeter and a range of different objects to find out how the mass of the object affects the force needed to get it moving. If you are using heavy objects, make sure you choose a suitable newtonmeter. If you are in any doubt, check with your teacher.

- Present your results in a table showing the mass of each object and the force needed to get it moving.

What do your results tell you?

Section 2.5
STOPPING

Generally, when you have got something moving you want to be able to stop it! To stop something moving you need a force. For example, you use brakes to stop a car or a bicycle moving. If the brakes don't work, then the car or bicycle will keep going until it smashes into something or it is stopped in some other way. In the following activity you are going to investigate the force needed to stop a car moving by letting a toy car or trolley run down a ramp into a barrier.

Investigate

- Devise a way of measuring the force which is needed to stop a toy car or trolley which is running down a ramp.

  Hint: Forces can change the shape of an object, such as the barrier the trolley runs into.

- Think about the force needed to stop a big, heavy car. Devise a way of investigating how the force needed to stop a car depends on its mass.

  Does a big, heavy car need a bigger force to stop it than a small, light car?

- Devise a way of investigating how the force needed to stop a car depends on how fast the car is moving.

runway

barrier

blocks or books to prop this end up

Section 2.6
BRAKES AND TYRES

Every year we hear reports of 'pile-ups' on the motorways, where several cars have been unable to stop before hitting the car in front of them.

Many people are killed and injured in road accidents each year

Think about

1 What do you think causes 'pile-ups'? What weather conditions make them more likely?

2 Look at the table on 'stopping distances', then answer these questions:

(a) Thinking distance is how far the car travels before the driver 'reacts', and seems to increase in a steady way as speed increases. What is the increase in thinking distance for every 10 kilometres per hour increase in speed?

(b) What would you expect to happen to the thinking distance as drivers become tired?

(c) Does the increase in braking distance follow the same pattern? Why do you think this is?

(d) Plot a graph of stopping distance in metres (vertical axis) against speed in kilometres per hour (horizontal axis). What would be the likely stopping distance at 120 kilometres per hour?

3 Drivers are advised to allow at least double the stopping distance in wet weather. Why do you think this is?

Stopping distances

Car speed (km/h)	Thinking distance (m)	Braking distance (m)	Total stopping distance (m)
30	5	5	10
40	7	10	17
50	9	15	24
60	11	22	33
70	13	30	43
80	15	38	53
90	17	48	65
100	19	60	79
110	21	73	94

4 The table gives the shortest likely stopping distances for a range of speeds in *good* conditions. How might the road surface or the weather affect stopping distances?

To stop a car you need good brakes and tyres. Careful car owners carry out regular checks to make sure that their brakes and tyres are in good condition. If the brake parts become worn they will not stop the wheels turning, and tyres with worn treads will not 'grip' the road surface correctly.

Tyres should be checked regularly and changed when the tread becomes worn

Section 2.7
FRICTION

Friction is a force between two surfaces that slows things down and makes sliding difficult; when there is not much friction, surfaces slide easily over each other. To stop a car, plenty of friction is needed between the brakes and the wheels, and also between the tyres and the road.

There is very little friction between the smooth blades of the skates and the ice

Investigate

• Find out what kinds of surfaces provide most friction and which provide the least by using a block and a board as shown in the diagram.

• Record how much the board has to be tilted before the block begins to slide.

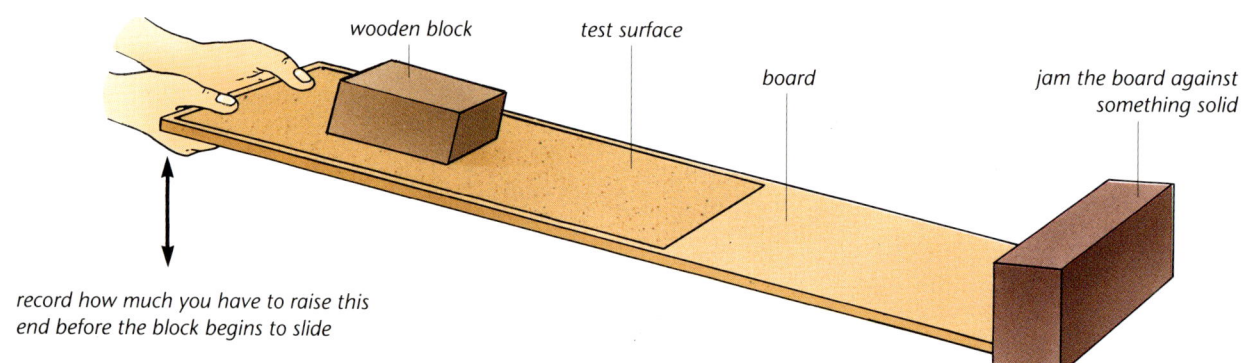

wooden block *test surface* *board* *jam the board against something solid*

record how much you have to raise this end before the block begins to slide

Sometimes, friction can be a nuisance and we use lubricants to try to reduce it. For example, door hinges and handles occasionally need oiling to stop them sticking or squeaking.

Think about

1 Which liquids can you use as a lubricant?

2 What would happen to a car engine if it was not properly lubricated?

3 Write down at least three situations where friction can be a nuisance and three more where it can be useful.

UNIT 3
SAFE JOURNEYS

Section 3.1
INERTIA

At some time or another, you have probably been standing inside a bus or train that has stopped suddenly, and found yourself hurtling forwards, along with everyone else who was standing! You carried on moving forwards because you had inertia. The inertia of a body is its tendency to resist changes in its movement. Inertia makes it difficult to start a body moving and difficult to stop it. The greater the mass of a body, the greater is its inertia. However, even objects with a small mass can have a lot of inertia if they are moving quickly. If a vehicle stops suddenly the objects inside it keep flying forwards. This can be dangerous even if the objects are quite small. They have a lot of inertia and can cause damage to anything they hit.

A ship has a large inertia – it is difficult for a ship to stop in a short distance

Think about

• What dangers does inertia present to passengers in fast-moving vehicles?

Section 3.2
SAFETY BELTS

One of the problems of travelling at higher speeds is that accidents are more damaging to the people, the vehicles and the objects involved in them. In an attempt to reduce the risk of injury to a car's occupants, the UK government has made a law about who must wear seat belts when they travel by car.

In this test crash, the driver was wearing a seat belt, but the back seat passenger, and the two children were not wearing seat belts

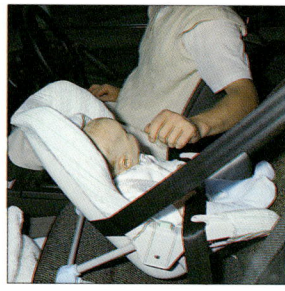
A car seat for a baby

A car seat for a young child

Research

- Find out the answers to the following questions:

  1 When must you wear a seat belt in a car?

  2 Do all cars have to have seat belts?

  3 Why is it important for everyone in a car to wear a seat belt?

  4 Besides providing seat belts, how can car manufacturers help to make the inside of a car safer for its occupants if it swerves or stops suddenly?

  5 Why is an adult seat belt not suitable for young children?

- Collect information and photographs about special safety fittings in cars for children. Find out what the recommended age or weight ranges are for each of the safety fittings, and how each of the different designs helps to restrain and protect a young child or baby. Make a display of the materials you have collected.

Think about

- Look at the safety seats shown in the two photographs. Some safety seats are fitted so that the baby faces backwards. What advantages would this give for a baby's safety if the car stopped suddenly?

  What other advantages might there be?

- If you were working for a consumers' organisation, evaluating seat belts for children, what features would you look for?

Section 3.3
CRUMPLE ZONES

udo contestants have to learn to fall correctly

The crumple zone of a car helps to protect the passengers from serious injury

It can really hurt when you jump off a wall or a piece of apparatus in the gym and land stiff-legged, but if you land correctly you make less noise and it doesn't hurt nearly as much! The difference is that when you land properly you stop yourself more slowly, so the stopping forces you experience are smaller.

Car manufacturers help to make cars safer for their occupants by designing them with 'crumple zones'. In a collision the bumpers and the front section of the car are meant to crumple on impact, so that the occupants are not stopped quite so suddenly. Even so, there is a limit to the protection that crumple zones can provide. Drivers sometimes drive faster because they think their cars are 'safe'. But injuries caused by crashes at high speed can be very serious, or even fatal.

Plan and test

- Plan an investigation to find the best design of a crumple zone for a laboratory trolley. Base your plan on the equipment shown in the diagram. Remember to consider the following points:

  What things must not change to make this a fair test?

  How will you make sure they stay the same?

  How will you compare the effectiveness of the crumple zones?

  What measurements could you make and record?

  What would be the best way to present your findings?

- When your plan has been approved, carry out your investigation and record your results.

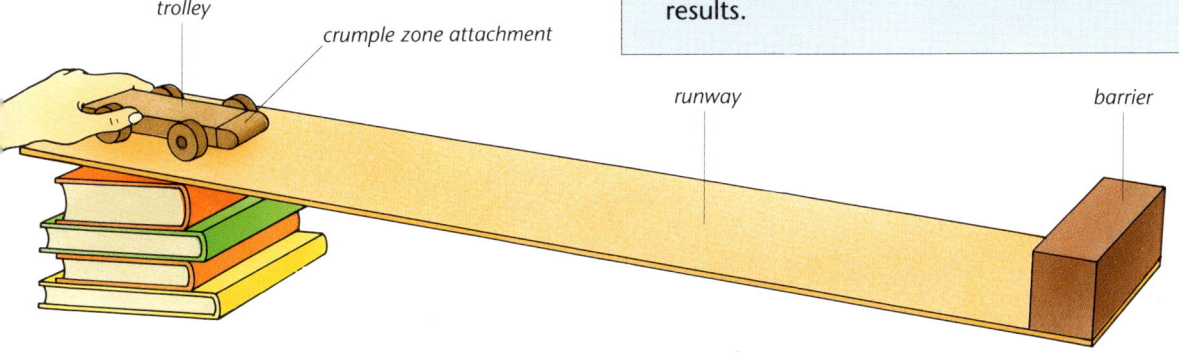

trolley

crumple zone attachment

runway

barrier

Section 3.4
TOPPLING TRANSPORTERS

Tractors are designed so that they can be used safely even on relatively steep slopes

A few years ago there were a number of serious accidents in which tractors being used on slopes toppled over and the roof of the driver's cab crumpled inwards, crushing the driver. In order to make the tractors safer, designers and manufacturers had to reduce the risk of the tractor toppling over and of the roof collapsing dangerously. These design considerations are also important for other vehicles: for example, the roofs of coaches are designed so that they don't collapse on the passengers if the coach rolls down an embankment. It is important for buses and lorries to be as stable as possible. The stability of buses is usually checked on a standard 'tilt table'.

Discuss

- The stability of a vehicle is affected by the way it is loaded. What else affects its stability?

- The push-along toy shown in this picture is very unstable. It would fall over easily and be dangerous for a toddler to play with.
If you were asked to design a push-along toy for a toddler, how would you change the design of the toy shown in the picture to make it less likely to fall over?

Investigate

- Investigate how changing the position of a load can affect the stability of a vehicle. Use a sweet tin or a similar container to represent the vehicle and some Plasticine to represent the load.

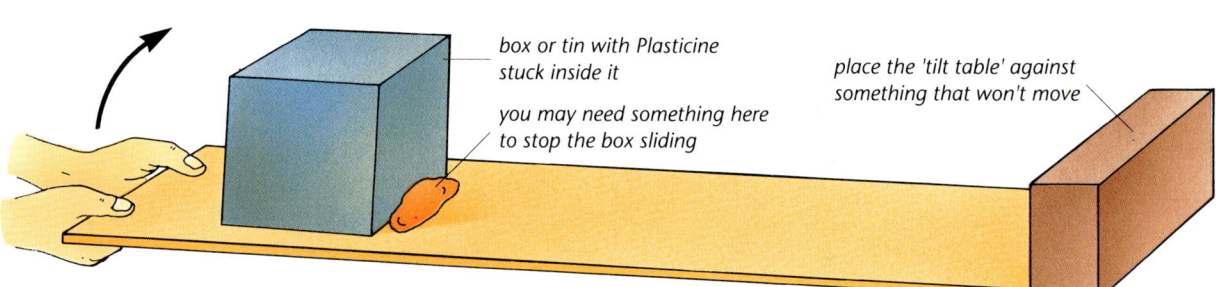

box or tin with Plasticine stuck inside it

you may need something here to stop the box sliding

place the 'tilt table' against something that won't move

raise this end until the box begins to fall over

UNIT 4
PROVIDING THE POWER

Section 4.1
WHAT MAKES IT GO?

We began this topic by looking at toy vehicles in the laboratory and thinking about what provided the force to make them move. In this unit we shall look at real vehicles and try to find out what makes them move.

All vehicles need a supply of energy to make them move; the muscles in your legs provide the energy to move a bicycle, while burning petrol provides the energy to make a car or motor bike move.

Of course, some cars and motor bikes seem more exciting than others. They are usually the ones with the most powerful engines. The more power an engine has, the faster the vehicle can accelerate (change speed) and the faster it burns up

Some motor bikes have very powerful engines. This shows Wayne Gardner on a 1123 cc Honda at Donington Park

the fuel! Powerful motors are important when vehicles need to climb steep hills or pull heavy loads, but they are not necessary if the vehicle has to travel along flat, even ground or transport light loads.

Research

• Look through books and magazines to find examples of, and information about, land, sea and air vehicles which rely totally or mainly on the following:

muscle power	oil
wind power	petrol
solar power	gas
batteries	other fuels
other electrical supply	

• Present your survey as a poster. Include on your poster written information, sketches and photographs.

Think about

• Look at each of the groups of vehicles in your survey, then write down your answers to these questions:

1 Are the vehicles used by a lot of people, or only a few?

2 Where are they used?

3 What are the advantages of using them?

4 What might be the problems or disadvantages?

5 Are any vehicles very new designs? What is special about them? Why have they only been made recently?

Section 4.2
MIXED-UP INVENTORS

Scientists often have to find out information to help them carry out their experiments more effectively. A lot of information can be found in libraries. You need to be able to use a library effectively to help you with your work in science and other subjects. The more often you use the library in your work, the easier it will be for you to find information quickly. The library activities which follow are an opportunity for you to practise your library skills as well as finding out about the work of some scientists and inventors.

Research

- Opposite are the names of six scientists and inventors whose work has led to developments in transport, and a brief description and picture of each person's achievements (A-F). Match the descriptions to the right people. Carry out research to find out which is the correct description for each person.

Hint: You could do this more easily and quickly if you share out the research amongst the people in your group and 'pool' your information.

The people

Carl Benz

Elijah McCoy   *Robert Goddard*

Igor Ivanovitch Sikorsky

Konstantin Tsiolkousky

George Stephenson

The descriptions

A The first person to produce a successful, single-rotor helicopter which could be made in quantity. (Twin-rotor helicopters had already been produced.)

A

B

D

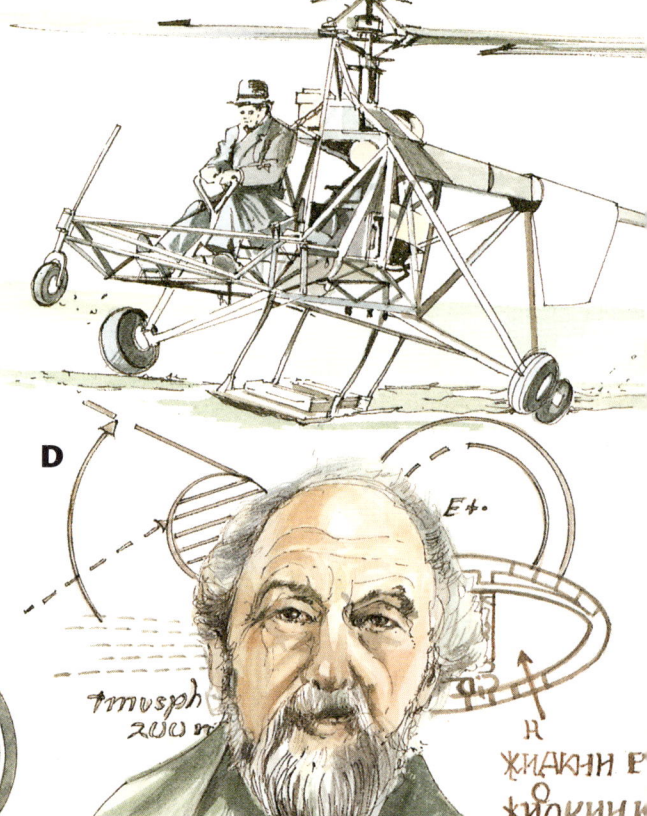

B Produced the first petrol-driven car (a three-wheeler capable of 16 kilometres per hour).

C The first person to design and produce a successful device that sent oil to a train engine automatically. Before this, trains had to break their journey so that the engine could be oiled. (The devices he made were so successful that his name became a byword for good quality.)

D Published a book on rocket motion which was used by later generations of rocket engineers. Although regarded as 'the father of space flight', he did not actually build any rockets himself.

E Carried out experiments on rocket flight and was the first person to produce a liquid fuel rocket which could travel faster than the speed of sound.

F He did not produce the first steam locomotive but improved a design by Richard Trevithick. His engine, 'The Locomotion', pulled the first goods train along the world's first stretch of public railway. His most famous engine, 'The Rocket', was the winner of speed trials which were held to choose a locomotive for a new passenger line between Manchester and Liverpool.

THE MARS MISSION: GETTING READY

Section 5.1
WELCOME TO THE SPACE ACADEMY!

Welcome to the Space Academy! My name is Io, and I'll be helping you with your assignments. As Space Cadets, you'll be working on the Mars Mission and you'll be asked to carry out several assignments so that a small exploratory team can land on Mars and do some experiments: your teacher will tell you which assignments you should attempt.

In order to complete these assignments you will need to use your knowledge of forces and speed, and your skills as an experienced scientist!

Don't worry if you can't do all of the assignments: some are quite hard to complete and don't have straightforward answers.

Good luck!

The planet Mars, as seen approaching it from space

During the Mars Mission, you will need to be in contact with Mission Control on Earth. Look at the information given in the data file entry; you will need to use it to work out how long it will take for messages to reach you from Earth during your journey.

DATA FILE ENTRY
RADIO CONTACT WITH MISSION CONTROL

There will be radio contact between the Mars team and Mission Control throughout the mission.
Radio waves are in the same 'family' of waves as light; all of them travel at 300 000 kilometres per second (1080 million kilometres per hour).

SUPPLEMENTARY DATA ENTRY
SPEED OF LIGHT

Speed is normally measured in metres per second (m/s) in the science laboratory, but very fast speeds may be measured in kilometres per second (km/s) or kilometres per hour (km/h).
Light travels at 300 000 kilometres per second. This tells you that
in 1 second it will travel
        300 000 kilometres;
in 2 seconds it will travel
        600 000 kilometres;
in 10 seconds it will travel
        3 000 000 kilometres.

Work out

1 The table shows the time it would take for a signal to reach you at different distances from Earth. Copy the table into your book and complete it by writing the numbers given below in the correct places.

Distance from Earth		Time for signal to arrive	
3 000 000	kilometres		
30 000 000	kilometres		
300 000 000	kilometres		
		1	second
		60	seconds
		120	seconds

18 000 000	kilometres	100	seconds
300 000	kilometres	1000	seconds
36 000 000	kilometres	10	seconds

2 Work out from the table how long it would take a message to reach you if you were:

(a) 6 million kilometres from Earth.

(b) 60 million kilometres from Earth.

(c) 600 million kilometres from Earth.

3 How far away would you be if the signal took:

(a) 1 second to reach you?

(b) 1 minute to reach you?

(c) 4 hours to reach you?

Work out   EXTRA!

• Spacecraft don't travel at the speed of light! Suppose the planned route to Mars is a journey of roughly 200 million kilometres: how long would it take to get there at an average speed of 40 000 kilometres per hour?

How long would it take at an average speed of 80 000 kilometres per hour?

Section 5.2
LAUNCH

Do you know how much you weigh? Imagine feeling three times as heavy! This is what it can feel like for astronauts as they are carried up away from Earth and into orbit.

Weight is the downward pull of the Earth on an object. If you want to lift something you have to pull upwards with at least as much force as the Earth is pulling downwards.

DATA FILE ENTRY
SHUTTLE LAUNCH

The first phase of the Mars Mission is a shuttle launch into low Earth orbit; once established in orbit, the shuttle craft will rendezvous with the Mars Probe for transfer of the Mars Mission crew.

Approximately 30 seconds after launch the shuttle will be travelling faster than the speed of sound (300 metres per second).

At about 500 seconds (eight or nine minutes) after launch the shuttle will be travelling at over 1 kilometre per second: this is about the right speed for maintaining orbit around the Earth.

The illustration shows the space shuttle system as developed by the US during the 1980s. It was the first re-usable spacecraft. It had successes – recapturing out of orbit satellites, and disasters – when the Challenger vehicle exploded in 1987.

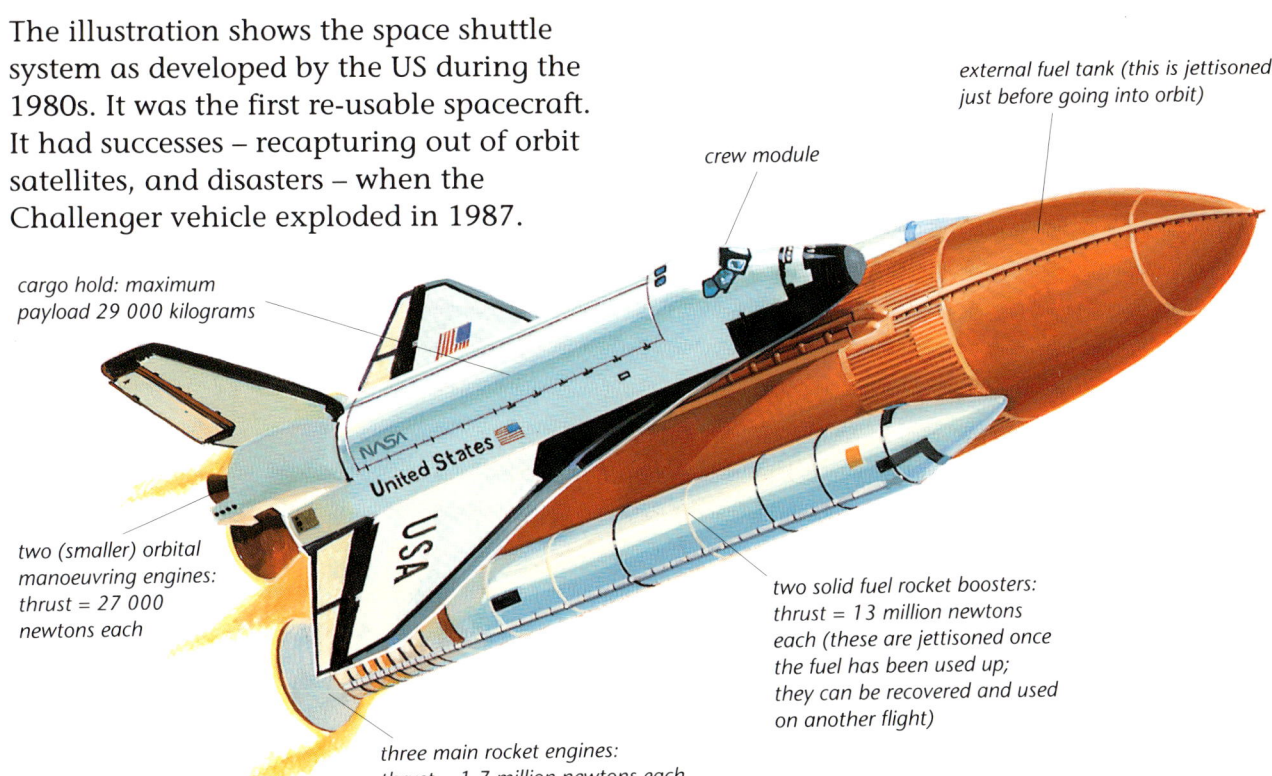

external fuel tank (this is jettisoned just before going into orbit)

crew module

cargo hold: maximum payload 29 000 kilograms

two (smaller) orbital manoeuvring engines: thrust = 27 000 newtons each

two solid fuel rocket boosters: thrust = 13 million newtons each (these are jettisoned once the fuel has been used up; they can be recovered and used on another flight)

three main rocket engines: thrust = 1.7 million newtons each

total mass at lift-off = 2 million kilograms

Investigate

- Hang a 1 kilogram mass from a forcemeter. The reading on the meter is the *weight* of the kilogram mass.

  How much force must you pull up with to just stop the kilogram mass from falling downwards?

  How much force would you need to just lift objects that weigh 20 newtons, 200 newtons and 1000 newtons?

- Now try pulling the forcemeter upwards sharply with the mass still attached. What happens to the reading as you start to pull?

  How does the weight of the object seem to change as you pull it up suddenly?

Work out

- Look at the diagram of the space shuttle above and answer these questions:

  1 What is the mass of the shuttle at launch?

  2 What is its weight?

  3 What force would be needed to just lift the shuttle?

  4 What total force do the engines and boosters provide?

  5 How much bigger is this force than the downward pull of the Earth?

Acceleration is how fast speed changes in a given time. For example, if from standing still you reach 10 metres per second (10 m/s) in 5 seconds, then your acceleration is 2 metres per second per second (2 m/s/s). That is, your speed increases by 2 metres per second every second.

Work out   EXTRA!

• Answer the following questions using the data file entry for the shuttle launch:

1 What is the average acceleration of the shuttle in the first 30 seconds?

2 What is the average acceleration in the first 500 seconds?

3 The greater the acceleration away from the Earth's surface, the heavier you feel. When would you feel the heaviest, in the first 30 seconds or as you approach orbiting speed?

Section 5.3
WEIGHT WATCHING

Many people think a person is weightless on the Moon and that there is no gravity in space. They are wrong!

Things on the Moon are not weightless, they just weigh less

What happens to the clubs if the clown drops them? What happens to them when he throws them in the air? Why?

DATA FILE ENTRY
GRAVITY, MASS AND WEIGHT

Mass is the 'amount of' something and is measured in kilograms. The mass of an object is the same no matter where the object is.

Gravity is a force that pulls objects together: you pull on the Earth and the Earth pulls you. The bigger the object, the stronger its pull on other objects, so you feel more of a 'pull down' - your weight - on Earth than you would feel on the Moon. On the other hand, Jupiter is a much larger planet than Earth so you would feel *much* heavier there.

Things are not weightless on the Moon, they just weigh less - and so would feel easier to lift. The force of gravity on Earth is 10 newtons on a mass of 1 kilogram (10 N/kg).

Think about

• Describe what you think a Space Olympics would be like on a planet where the pull of gravity was much less than on Earth.

Which events would be easier?

Would spectators in an air-conditioned stadium dome on the Moon be safe during javelin throwing if they sat as far away from the event as they would do on Earth?

Section 5.4
WHEN WILL I BE WEIGHTLESS?

When you are travelling at a steady speed, far away from any planets or stars, you will be weightless.

It can take a little time to get used to being weightless, as just a small push can send you or your equipment gliding off to the other end of the cabin or into a spin. Weightlessness means there is no 'up' or 'down' any more: if you let go of something it won't fall to the floor, but it won't float off to the ceiling either; any spilt liquid or crumbs from your meal will just hang around until you can catch them all!

Think about

- Look at the cartoons of life on board the starship 'Improbable'.
  Do they show things you might expect to happen during weightlessness or not?
  If not, why not?
  How might they be possible?
  Write down your answers.

Section 5.5
LONG-TERM WEIGHTLESSNESS

DATA FILE ENTRY
EFFECTS OF LONG-TERM WEIGHTLESSNESS

Research evidence to date suggests that long stays in low gravity or zero gravity can cause bones and muscles to weaken.

Observe and record

- Measure the strength of your own muscles by pushing on to bathroom scales in the three positions shown in the diagram.

- Which 'test' needs most force? Which the least? What was the strongest grip? What was the weakest?

- Present a survey of your group or class results.

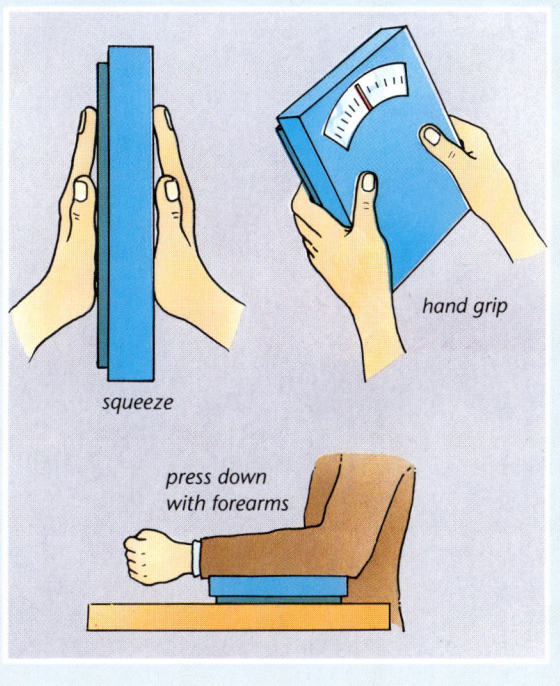

squeeze

hand grip

press down with forearms

Research

- Many astronauts have now experienced weightlessness for several days at a time and have carried out lots of experiments while weightless. Find out how they cope with everyday tasks while weightless. For example, how do they eat, drink, wash or go to the toilet?

American astronauts experiencing weightlessness in space

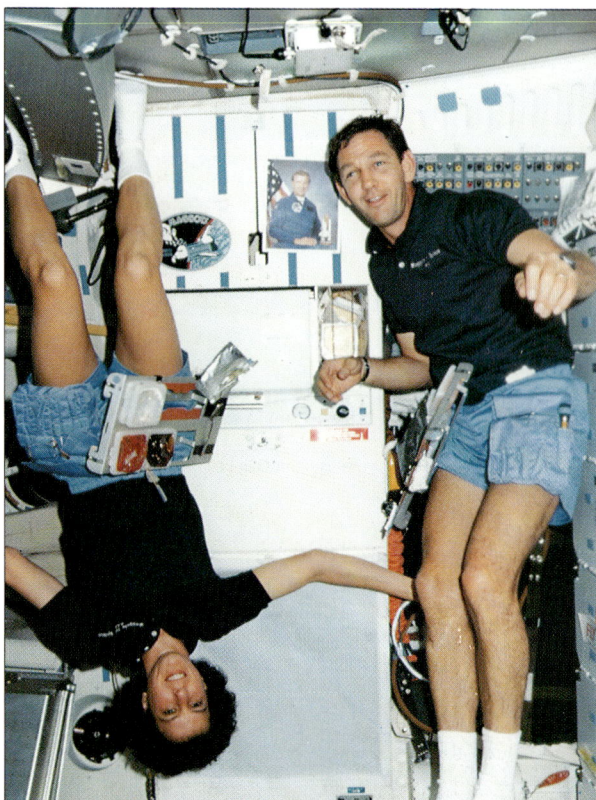

Plan

- Design a device (or several devices) to measure muscle strength for an astronaut in low or zero gravity.

- Present your ideas on how astronauts could try to prevent their muscles weakening.

Which is the better method?   *...like this...*   *...or like this*

THE MARS MISSION: ARRIVAL AND RETURN

Section 6.1
INTERPLANETARY FLIGHT

aerial for messages to/from Earth

launch pad

feet for landing (normally folded away)

solar panels to provide electricity

landing module

fuel tanks

thrusters for manoeuvring

NASA

antennae for use in docking

crew area

DATA FILE ENTRY
THE MARS PROBE

The Space Shuttle will take cadets to a space station. This is in orbit beyond the Earth's atmosphere. From here, cadets will board the Probe, for the journey to Mars.

The Mars Probe is not like the Space Shuttle or traditional rockets. The Shuttle is streamlined whereas the Mars Probe has antennae and solar panels sticking out. The Shuttle and traditional rockets have huge fuel tanks, whereas the Mars Probe just has large fuel tanks for the landing module, and only needs small rocket motors to adjust its speed and direction during the rest of the journey.

The Probe is travelling very fast. Why don't all the bits that are sticking out snap off? Why doesn't the Probe need huge fuel tanks for such a long journey?

Plan and test

- Use a ruler to flick a coin across different flat surfaces as shown in the diagram. Measure the stopping distance on each surface.

  How will you try to make this a fair test?

- Record your results in a table or bar chart.

  What pattern do you notice in your results?

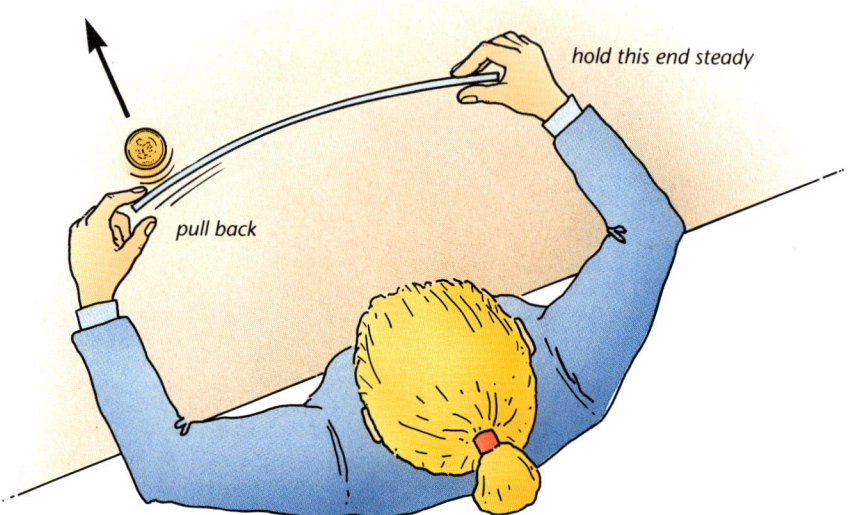

pull back

hold this end steady

Discuss

- Why do you think that things slow down and stop on Earth if you don't keep pushing them, but in space things keep going at the same speed.

Think about   **EXTRA!**

- Some science fiction writers think that journeys to the outer planets of the solar system could be made using 'constant boost' rockets. 'Constant boost' rockets produce a constant push and hence a constant acceleration. This means that the speed will keep on increasing. In fact, it has been suggested that with a constant acceleration of 0.1 g (about 1 metre per second per second), a spacecraft could reach Pluto in just 50 days!

- Why would 'constant boost' spacecraft not use conventional chemically powered rockets?

Section 6.2
THE LANDING

DATA FILE ENTRY
PLANETARY SURFACE AT
LANDING SITE

Data currently available suggests that the surface of the landing area on Mars (chosen for being fairly flat) may be sandy and quite soft. Any landing modules and exploratory vehicles must not sink too far into the surface as it could prove difficult to get them out.

View of Mars from Viking 1

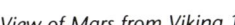

Investigate

- Use a tripod and sand tray as shown in the diagram to investigate how the load you use and the area of the feet affect the depth of the 'footprint'.

- Present your findings in a table or bar chart.

- Use your findings to suggest which of the feet shown in this diagram would be the best shape for the landing module. Give reasons for your choice.

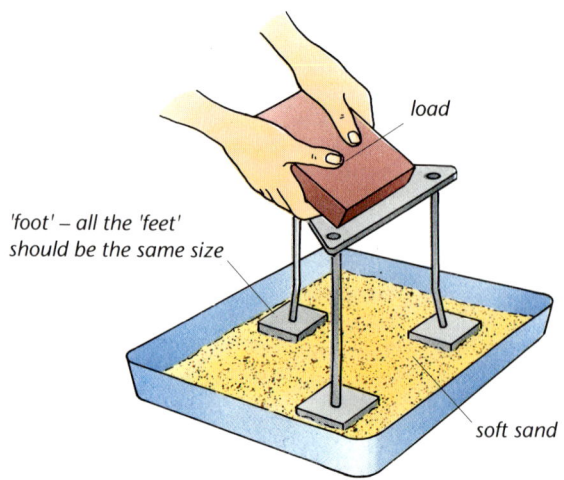

load

'foot' – all the 'feet' should be the same size

soft sand

spikes

small, square ended feet

large circular feet

Plan

- Draw a simple design for the wheels and frame of an exploratory vehicle to be used on Mars.

Research   **EXTRA!**

- People and animals need to travel across soft surfaces such as snow and sand here on Earth. Find out how the shape of their feet (or shoes) helps them to avoid sinking into the surface.

People wear snow shoes to make it easier to walk over snowy surfaces

Section 6.3
SURFACE CONDITIONS

A small group of cadets and Mars scientists have to set up an experiment several kilometres from the landing site. They must carry equipment to the site and set it up. They do not need to bring the equipment back as the experiment will run for several months. The data from the experiment will be transmitted directly to Earth.

> ### DATA FILE ENTRY
> #### SURFACE CONDITIONS ON PLANNED ROUTE
>
> This area has not been previously explored, but satellite surveys suggest that conditions along the planned route will vary as shown on the map.

Plan and test

- Design and carry out a fair test to compare how easy it is to slide objects across different kinds of surface.

  Which surfaces provide the most *friction* (make movement difficult) and which provide the least?

- Present your findings in a table or bar chart.

- Look again at the planned route on the map.

  What would you expect to be some of the problems in moving across the glassy regions?

  How would you try to overcome these problems?

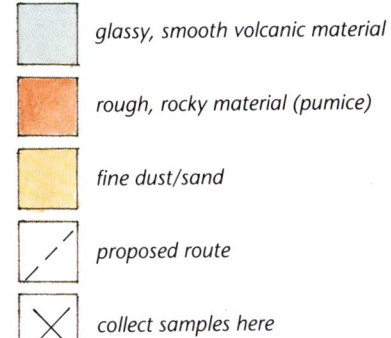

glassy, smooth volcanic material

rough, rocky material (pumice)

fine dust/sand

proposed route

collect samples here

Section 6.4
THE VOYAGE HOME

Once all planned activities on Mars have been completed, the Mars crew will leave the planet in the landing module. After docking with the orbiting Probe has been safely completed they will leave Mars' orbit for the return journey to Earth. The Mars Probe is designed for inter-planetary travel and cannot land on Earth. Instead, the Probe crew will transfer to a space shuttle at a space station orbiting hundreds of kilometres above the Earth, far beyond the limits of the atmosphere.

The next data file entry shows you how complicated their return will be.

Why can't the astronauts just return to Earth in the Probe?

DATA FILE ENTRY
RE-ENTRY AND LANDING

The shuttle will leave the space station and go into a lower orbit, still beyond the atmosphere, until it is cleared to begin re-entry. To do this, the pilot turns the shuttle round until it is facing backwards, then he fires the orbital engines to slow it down. As the shuttle is no longer travelling fast enough to stay in orbit it begins to fall to Earth.

The shuttle enters the Earth's atmosphere 'nose up' so that the air hitting the underside helps to slow the fall. Friction from the air also causes the shuttle to heat up, particularly round the nose and leading edges of the wings. To fly the shuttle in the atmosphere, the pilot must fly it as though it were a glider. He cannot make use of the orbital manoeuvring engine any more. This also means that there can only be one attempt at landing, and this will be like landing a jet aircraft without engines. The pilot puts the shuttle into a steep swoop to land like a glider, only much faster. As the shuttle touches down, the pilot pulls the nose up again and the rudder opens like a book to act as an air brake. It takes several kilometres of runway for the shuttle to slow down and stop.

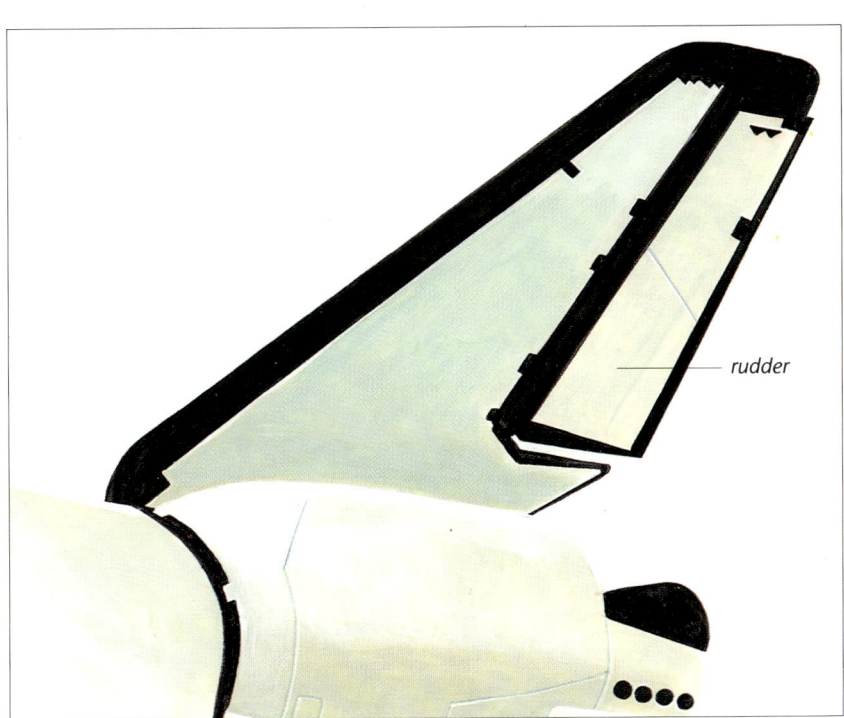

rudder

Rudder action: one piece swinging from side to side

rudder

Air brake action: the two sections of the rudder split apart

Space shuttle re-entering the atmosphere

Think about

- Make a list of all the methods used to slow down the shuttle.

- Parachutes are generally used to make things fall more slowly. Why are parachutes not used in this case?

Design   EXTRA!

- The shuttle is covered in special materials to withstand the heat of re-entry. These include special ceramic tiles and a material called carbon-carbon, which can withstand even higher temperatures than the tiles. Draw a picture of the shuttle showing where you would use each of these materials.